The Phelps Family and the Wine Trade in 19th Century Madeira

The Story from their Letters

ANTHEA BOYLSTON AND
PENELOPE FORREST

DEDICATION

This volume is dedicated to all the descendants of Joseph and Elizabeth Phelps of Madeira

Cover photograph: Lithograph of Quinta do Prazer at Monte drawn by Andrew Picken in 1842.

The photograph of Frances Hubbard is published by kind permission of Judith Hubbard and the picture of Curral das Freiras by permission of the Bodleian Library, Oxford.

CONTENTS

ACKNOWLEDGMENTS

We are extremely grateful to Cláudia Faria for all the work she has carried out on the history of our family, which has been generously shared with us. We have developed a wonderful collaboration with Judith Hubbard in our study of the Phelps and their time in Madeira. Thanks are due to Martin and Rachel Shirley for finding another cache of letters just recently and to Christopher Morgan-Smith for giving us the lithograph of Quinta do Prazer.

Preface

Anthea Boylston and Penelope Forrest are both triple great granddaughters of William and Elizabeth Phelps, who began this story in the 1770s. The family letters are well-travelled. Their initial survival is remarkable since they had to journey between Madeira and England as well as between Madeira and India. Many of them were then brought home by their recipient, Lieutenant General Arthur Phelps, when he eventually retired from the Bombay Army in the 1890s. The letters were preserved by his grandchildren. Some went to Sicily after the Second World War where they were kept by Daphne Phelps at her villa in Taormina. We found them there after her death in 2005. Others were contained in a trunk in the attic of a Sussex stable. The earliest missives recently emerged from a drawer in the Somerset home of Martin and Rachel Shirley.

The letters were scanned and emailed to Penelope in South Africa. She then transcribed the often illegible Victorian script and the story of a family emerged. Penelope had already established a very fruitful collaboration with Cláudia Faria in Madeira, where our family is still remembered. The extracts quoted here are published in more detail in *A Shoebox of Letters* by Penelope Forrest, Anthea Boylston and Judith Hubbard. Much further information about the wider family can be found on Judith's website hubbardplus.co.uk and on phelps-ancestry.co.uk.

1 INTRODUCTION

William Phelps left London on 18ᵗʰ January 1784 with his new wife Elizabeth and sailed for Madeira. His family had lived at Dursley in Gloucestershire for generations. William had already started producing and exporting wine with James Morrisey in Madeira during the 1770s. When William set off for the island, his brother Joseph took over the London end of the business, and the partnership was formalised by an agreement in 1790.

William and Elizabeth had three daughters and four sons, all born in Madeira, and William built Carmo House which still stands opposite the Carmo Church in Funchal. The family lived above the business premises (always referred to as the "counting house"). In 1800 Joseph died and William had to find another partner. The person he chose was the husband of his oldest daughter Eliza, Robert Page, who already lived in Madeira. Their partnership was established in 1803 and became extremely successful. In May 1805, by which time William has returned to England with his wife and two other daughters to run that end of the business, Robert Page acquired the Quinta do Prazer in Monte above the town at a very good price. This is now the renowned Tropical Gardens.

Three of William and Elizabeth's sons followed their father into the family business and it was the third son, Joseph (his uncle's namesake) who with his wife and family, spent most of his life on the

Island where they played an important part in the community. All the boys had been educated in England, and there Joseph met Elizabeth Dickinson whom he married in 1819. His proposal reads like a Jane Austen novel:

Madeira 16 October 1818

My dear Eliza,

Under an infatuated certainty that you will meet the wishes of this letter, I take the liberty of thus addressing you. Circumstances would not allow of my mentioning, when I had the pleasure of seeing you at Bramblebury, what now through this medium I mean to communicate to you, & hope, should this letter offend you, you will pardon the writer & cast it into the fire.

When in England last, I had determined to do my utmost to ally myself to some lady, in whose company I might hope to pass the remainder of my days happily, and at the same time to cause the happiness of her with whom I might be fortunate enough to unite myself. In you, I think I have found that lady and if I am not too presumptuous, and your affections are not previously engaged, I beg most earnestly to make you an offer of my hand and heart, which I sincerely hope you will accept & trust that you will never have reason to repent having done so. You will no doubt be aware of the difficulty a person labours under in writing a letter on such a subject as the present, & accordingly forgive the stiffness of style in which it must appear written.

I will not now trouble you farther on the subject until I have the pleasure of hearing from you, which I hope will be soon, with a confirmation of my wishes. I have farther to request that you will for the present, communicate this only to your Father & Mother; no other person should know it, not even your Brothers or Sisters. I <u>beg</u> you to comply with my request. Should I receive a favourable answer, I will then write to my own family when I am confident every thing will be arranged to the satisfaction of all parties. Adieu my dear Eliza & in hopes of the best I remain

Yours ever truly

Joseph Phelps

Joseph brought his bride home to Madeira in the summer of 1819 and in October she wrote to her sister, Anne Evans in England:

"How I wish you & Arthur could see this beautiful island, if only for a few days. The mountains <u>come against the sky</u> in a manner that would astonish him, as the air is so rarified as to enable you to see such distant objects quite distinctly, and you cannot help fancying that the trees etc are actually small because you see them plainly when their distance diminishes them so much. Such scenery is exactly adapted for painting, and the climate would enable him to sketch all day long. I have not yet seen any of his favourite Gamboge tints however nor are there any cows grazing on the Hills, but in many places the soil is of a bright Red Ochre, which affords a contrast with the greenness of the vineyards around as pleasing to my eye, as anything in our Gravel pit. Among the minor beauties that my short walks have enabled me to notice I have observed hedges of Fucia (I don't know whether that is the way to spell it) and china Roses, and as shade seems

3

to be the chief object considered in laying out a garden here, you always see plenty of Trellis work, over which the Cobea & other creepers that are rarities with us, flourish in a state of nature. Indeed such things are no rarities here. I think the Orange & Palm are the most beautiful of the trees."

This booklet is based largely on letters exchanged between Joseph and his wife as well as many written to their youngest son Arthur, while he was at school in England or serving in the Bombay Army in India. Elizabeth's sister, Anne Dickinson (recipient of the above letter), had married the Reverend Arthur Benoni Evans who was Headmaster of Market Bosworth School in Leicestershire. Arthur Phelps, as his older brothers had done, attended this school, living with his aunt, uncle and cousins, seeing his parents and siblings only when they visited England. A few of the extracts also come from letters written to Arthur by his seven sisters and three brothers.

Elizabeth, known as Bella to distinguish her from her mother, was the eldest daughter and is remembered in Madeira for her work in promoting the embroidery industry abroad. She was followed by Mary, Anne (known also as Kitty), Frances (known as Fanny), Harriet, Joseph, Clara, Charley, Willy, Arthur and Janey. All the girls were very musical and their talents were put to good use at the various social events which formed such a big part of life in the English community. Their characters and later lives are described in Chapter

11.

Cláudia Faria has published a book based on her MA dissertation on the story of the Phelps family in Madeira and their role in the wine trade. However, this is available only in Portuguese so it is hoped this booklet will tell part of their story for interested English speakers and also explain why the name of Phelps is still honoured in Madeira today.

Carmo House in Funchal

2 BUSINESS

In 1790, when William Phelps first set up his wine shipping business with his brother Joseph and James Morrisey, there were already more than 30

British companies involved in the Madeira wine trade. By 1828 this number had increased to 71 but successive outbreaks of disease in the vines meant that by 1880 the number of Houses had been reduced to fewer than 20[1].

In 1805 the Napoleonic Wars were reaching their zenith and the war at sea was to have a considerable effect on trade in the island. This would prove difficult for all the merchants, in particular the very successful business that the partnership between William Phelps and Robert Page had achieved.

In February 1805 Robert writes to William in London: "A little Prize sent in here by the *Egyptienne* Frigate sails I understand this morning for England & affords me the present opportunity of writing. Our weather has been so unsettled that since I last wrote, the *Elbe* was for two days & a half in the utmost danger of going on the Beech, and is now at sea with the loss I imagine of another Anchor & Cable; several other vessels are also out of Port. The *Euryalus* Frigate has also been here, & the Captain assures us that the King in his speech to Parliament, mentions some overtures of Peace, having been made by the French, which is joyful news, & we trust it will end in this desired effect. Madeira continues as if all the Island was besieg'd: the Ports all mann'd & arm'd with everything for attack or defence – all the People called out without ceasing, and very often labour entirely stopp'd from the Preparations & exercising that are going forwards. We hear that all this is against Troops of any nation that attempt to come here,

& as there seems a certainty of English ones being the first, we may chance to see some unpleasant scene take place, if they persist in their obstinacy of keeping off British Men of War.

"Flour, I am happy, sells brisk at 2$500 & 2$600 per arrove and as it costs twelve dollars per Barrel, just now in America, I think there is as little chance of its lowering, as there is of any more being imported. We have I make sure this moment on hand full 3000 Barrels, on which the Present Rise will make a difference of about 10,000$, which is a pleasing addition of the Profits that calculated on for the last Year.

"Having occasion to fine down forty Pipes of Wine for Mr. Le Gros the owner of the Brig *Ceres* that you recommended to the House some time since, Miguel Ferreira made use of Isinglas, and in three days the operation was effected, rendering the Wine not only beautiful in appearance but giving it a rich Taste, and I think it will be an excellent Plan to keep always by us some Pipes to ship for Bill orders & anything very particular."

Robert continues to extol the good fortune of the company in the same letter: "You will be gratified, as well as myself, with the assurances I can give you that we are Reckon'd the most fortunate House of any in the Island & I have numberless congratulations from friends here; tho' they would give me very little pleasure did I not know the flourishing state we are in, better than anyone else. You now, I trust, have plenty of money in England & are perfectly happy; I see nearly £11,000 have gone home in Bills since Octr 7 tho' some of them are at a long date, we can reckon with a certainty, that it is Property well dispos'd of."

Unfortunately Robert was unduly optimistic about the prospects of peace with France and it was not until the Battle of Trafalgar in October that Nelson's fleet defeated the French and Spanish so trade could resume uninterrupted.

William's son Joseph joined the company in 1814 and took over the Madeira end of the business when Robert Page and his wife later moved to England. He carried on the business successfully for the following 40 years with his brothers William and Charles forming the London end of operation.

As well as wine, the family firm traded in various other commodities with mixed success. While Joseph was in England in 1847, his wife writes: "Bayman thinks that you might do very well with a cargo of breadstuffs here, provided you bought it cheap, ½ cash & ½ wine, for which the glut in England may perhaps present a favourable opp[y]. 2000 Moyos Milho[2] & Flour came in during the month of Aug[st] & they are still coming.

"Bayman hopes that James[3] has written to you to recommend you to send out Sovereigns. He says that all the 10 years he has been here, he never remembers money being so scarce. James has sent me some bills (£50) to sign, saying that tho' he did not want the money, he thought it best to take the bill when Boldering offered it, as it is almost impossible to get Bills.

"James has had no luck with the Rice. Bayman advises we sell it all at 1700R, if possible, but even this has not yet been effected. The Crackers do not go off at all, so all we can hope is that the profits on the flour may atone for the losses in the other articles. The sale of the Hats was excellent."

Life was not always easy but the Phelpses managed to make a reasonable living. However, the necessity for providing dowries for several of their daughters definitely strained the family finances. In July 1851, Elizabeth writes to Joseph:

"The orders for 4 & ¼ pipes in the letter to James, were a welcome addition, & very encouraging. It is remarkable how many of your customers are Rev^{ds}. Do not go on your way with a heavy heart; you have really no reason. John may wish you had turned to the Sherry trade, but I am quite content with the Madeira. It has always afforded you eno' to maintain us in comfort & plenty (in addⁿ to what we have) & I trust in God it always will, & there is every reason to think so. I know how difficult you must find it to obtain orders, but still they do drop in f^m time to time, & you must take it easy when you are disappointed."

Things were about to change drastically. In 1851 a mildew disease *Oidium tuckeri*, arrived in Madeira in some specimens belonging to a French botanist. It spread rapidly throughout the vines on the island and by November 1852 people were beginning to try other crops, as one of the letters reports: "As far as I have heard there seems to be little prospect of the vines recovering themselves for some time.

All vegetation seems to be undergoing some change. You know that the potato blight has never been cured & I think it seems to have recovered itself less in Madeira than elsewhere. Some crops of potatoes this year have quite failed. Many of the country people have rooted up the vines & I think it was wise of them for it is at all events more likely that other crops will do, than that the vines should go on as usual next year. But I think that those who can afford it, would do well to wait & see the event & even if they do again fail they will not feel it so much as the poor people who have only that to depend upon.

"Some wonderful batatas (sweet potatoes) do you remember them? have been brought here from Demarara. About a year ago a man brought 3 of these with him & the people say that it is better than if he had brought 3000 dollars. They are now planted all over the island & yield 3 crops a year whereas the ones we are accustomed to only bear once a year. It is a sort of convolvulus & has a beautiful flower & leaf."

In a letter of November 1853, Joseph writes: "As to Vintages we must give up all thoughts of them. The people are turning their attention to the cultivation of Sugar Canes & the rearing of Cochineal, which Canarians have found a most profitable substitute for their Vines, which since the disease they have rooted out."

And in March 1856, Elizabeth tells her son that "There is no prospect of any more wine here, but quantities of Sugar Canes are grown instead. They do not pay however when made into Sugar, & the consequence is, that the Island is filled with an ordinary spirit, between rum & brandy, which I fear will have the effect of deteriorating the character of the people."

Not only had the production of new wine dried up, but Madeira wine declined in popularity and the Phelpses had difficulty selling the wine they had on hand. In 1860 Joseph & Elizabeth with Bella and Janey moved to England, leaving the Baymans in Carmo House, the only members of the family still on the island.

William and Elizabeth Phelps

3 EMBROIDERY

The craft of embroidery and lace-making is thought to have arrived on the island with the early Portuguese settlers in the fifteenth century, when it was the preserve of noblewomen. It was certainly practised by nuns in the convents. Bella (Elizabeth) Phelps realised how unique it was and would teach the techniques to orphans in Santana.

One of her mother's letters, written in 1858, explains in detail that though "Madeira-work" had long been a cottage industry on the island, Bella's very valuable role had been in bringing the work to a much wider market. She took some samples to London in the 1840s where the embroidery became popular with Queen Victoria and her ladies-in-waiting. Some examples of Madeira white lace were exhibited at the Great Exhibition of 1851 leading to a great increase in its popularity, especially for weddings.

"She (Bella) has been a negro slave to the "bordados"[4] and has passed through severe anxiety in the promotion of this important article of benefit to the Island. When she first undertook to beg her friends in England to dispose of the works of several poor young women here whom she had been in the habit of assisting with her taste and skill, she did not at all foresee the extent to which the laws of "demand" and "supply" would lead. She soon found herself in the difficulty of having got beyond her command of money. The poor starving girls whose work she was recommending in England, could not, of course, wait for payment until it was sold there. She paid them the instant they finished it (often before) by dint of borrowing of her friends.

"The Papa and Robert both helped her, but explained, at the same time, how "kindness must be business". Jack Evans, simultaneously recommended that the ladies in England who laboured so generously in disposing of the work, should be protected from loss by a fixed commission, and Bella then beginning to systematize, has gone on from step to step till the whole aspect of the peasantry in this neighbourhood is completely changed. Instead of the mean, starved, ragged drudges that the female population used to appear, they now look like well fed and well clothed country women, and it is all owing to "Bordados".

"It is not only Bella who employs them, many trades people, both English and Portuguese, have taken up the trade to greater or less extent, but it is Bella who pays them best and most quickly and who assists them most with instruction and fashion. They therefore importune her for employment as much as ever, and she gives it to about 500. Every month she sends to England a box by Packet, containing about £200 to 250 worth of embroidery all paid for, and the box returns the following month filled with materials viz muslins from Glasgow, Lawns from Belfast, Thread from Belper, patterns from Paris. All this requires a large organisation, and it is a marvel to me, how Bella has effected it. She is nearly out of debt, in spite of several losses. One, of about £10 worth of embroidery ordered by a lady on the coast of Africa, whose husband was a bankrupt when it arrived.

"Uncle Charles has been very kind in acting as Banker, and not minding being a little overdrawn. The ladies in different parts of England who used to find the burden of postages, carriages, parcels delivery and bad debts intolerably burdensome, are able to renew their endeavours now they are protected from loss, and Bella herself is relieved from the danger of injuring her friends by her endeavours to benefit strangers. The manual labours however (equally shared now by Clara) continue to increase, but she is able to execute them with an easy mind.

"The system of pattern drawing is very pretty. They (your Sisters) "bone out" the pattern mathematically themselves, then prick through some dozens or hundreds of papers with fine needles (headed of course) so as to give centres for compasses. These, they pass on to several girls whom they have taught to use the compasses, and to do other parts of the drawing out, which they do with a dexterity which would astonish people accustomed only to the awkwardness of the English poor. Some few of them can copy <u>any</u> pattern, <u>by the eye</u> with a precision perfectly surprising and can even originate a collar, or adapt it from a straight pattern. If Bella never were to do any further good in the world than to put this means of an honest livelihood into so many female hands, she would not have lived in vain. The Lancastrian School[5] was formerly dedicated to teaching only <u>plain</u> work, but we have now introduced "bordados" as being more profitable, and I am learning of Clara, all the best methods of forming rules for the art. Bella, mean time, is able to pay her own expenses in England out of her profits, and when she shall be quite free of her early advances, will honestly deserve to make an honest penny herself by the fruit of toil and anxiety for others."

Frances Hubbard, Elizabeth's great niece dressed in Madeira lace.

4 CHURCH AFFAIRS

Madeira, as a province of Portugal, was entirely Roman Catholic but the large British Protestant community raised funds to build an English church which was opened in 1822. The Reverend Richard Lowe arrived in Madeira in 1826, mostly interested in studying the flora and fauna, but in 1831 he undertook to do locum duties for the English chaplain who went on leave. There was already some ill feeling surrounding the post as the rich businessmen who had raised the funds to build the church wished to dictate matters.

Real trouble flared up when Lowe became interested in the very high church Oxford Movement and was accused by some of introducing "Popish practices". The resident English community became sharply divided, with the Phelps family continuing to side with Lowe and Mary Phelps regularly playing the organ for services. The situation was further complicated by the arrival in Madeira of colourful Reverend John Mason Neale in February 1843. He and Reverend Edward Landon would become staunch allies of Lowe and when Neale and Landon were seen to attend a service in the Roman Catholic cathedral in Funchal, Lowe's enemies were incensed.

When Joseph visits England in 1847, Elizabeth's letters to him are full of news of the intrigue. Here is a sample:

"We are utterly dismayed by a letter Mr Lowe has received from the Bishop, advising him to resign, thus giving the whole weight of his episcopal support to the voluntary system and the factious portion of the inhabitants, for, recollect, they have always professed that what they wanted was for him to resign. This advice is coupled with something else which prevents him from shewing the letter, which was probably designedly done on the Bishop's part as he did not want his shuffling unworthy conduct to be made public. The "something else" is a most cruel censure upon Mr Lowe's conduct, made upon the authority of a person whom he does not name. He says "he fears Mr Lowe has not acted in the spirit of his advice, not to give needless offence, for he is told by a person who has resided some time in Madeira, that in all his services, especially the administration of the Holy Communion both <u>public</u> and <u>private</u>, he <u>conveys the impression</u> that he leans more to the doctrines of the Church of Rome than of England and that in the Holy Communion he <u>appears</u> to believe that the body and blood of Christ to be corporally present under the form of bread and Wine and that in general he <u>seems</u> to entertain a preference for Romanism and a dislike of Protestantism. And that his opponents are the great majority of the most <u>high-principled</u> and <u>respectable</u> of the Merchants here. This unknown slanderer can be no other than our friend Dyster."

Later she writes to Joseph:

"You are right in thinking it was not Dyster who maligned Lowe to the Bp. It was Scott Surtees, as the Bishop tells him in his last letter. I think a more unworthy act from one Clergyman – say Gentleman – to another could not be perpetrated. I am very sorry for it as I foresee it will ultimately engender a coolness between the Hamonds and us, which I should sincerely deplore."

In November 1847 Lord Palmerston, British Foreign Secretary, dismissed Lowe and appointed a Reverend Brown to the post, but the Bishop of London, under whose licence the chaplain acted, refused to grant a licence to Brown. When he arrived in 1848, Lowe and some of his parishioners including the Phelpses, left to establish a rival church in the Becco das Aranhas.

Both churches continued to operate but in 1851 there were still rumblings and one of

Elizabeth's letters of that year reports:

"The less satisfactory communication is the Church news, which however, is not so bad as Bewicke represents. It leaves us much in the position in which we were before, for, far from desiring Mr Lowe to give up, the Bishop contemplates both the clergymen in Madeira and will be ready to give his advice and admonitions to either".

By October 1851, Elizabeth writes: "Our Church news is rather encouraging. Mr Kenyon, Mr Gladstone, Lord Nelson[6] and Lord Lyttleton all write that there can be no doubt that our right course is to go on quietly and steadily, on the Bishop's promise to extend his "customary jurisdiction" over us; and saying that the Society in England will assist us to pay Mr Lowe's successor[7]. A Clergyman has already applied for the situation, but it is not known whether he will do. There is a Mr Hosmer come for his wife's health, being perfectly well himself."

In April 1855 a letter contains the news that "M^r and Mrs Lowe are in the Island. We enjoy their society very much, and it is refreshing to hear some good music again.

"I am sorry to say we are likely to lose Mr Hosmer. His wife has been very ill of late, and seems to require a further change. If he goes, the Bishop is not likely to give a licence to anybody else, so that I fear we shall be forced to amalgamate with the other Congregation. It will be a great grief to lose all our beautiful Services and Gregorian Chants."

Mr Hosmer was, however, followed by Mr Dorsey, both of whom were friends of the Phelps family and gave lessons to their children. In

September John Crompton writes that "Mr Dorsey's school gets on pretty well. He has applied to his Bishop, viz of Glasgow, to give him a licence to officiate for us in which case the building in the Rua das Aranhas will be continued."

In December 1855, Elizabeth writes to her son, "Do you know we are in hopes that all the difficulties of the Madeira Church question are about to be overcome. It seems highly probable that the Bishop of London will, when he gets well (he is very ill at this moment I grieve to say) institute a Clergyman to our congregation, which is all we ask, having not the least intention or inclination to interfere with any other, or to revive controversy or discussion. In the mean time, the Church Wardens have requested Mr Crompton to officiate provisionally, which he is doing, when his throat permits."

In May 1860, in another letter to Arthur, she says: "We have passed a very happy winter, with many agreeable friends and plenty of Music. The last 2 Months the Lowes have been staying with us, to avoid the Spring in England which always lays up Mr L. He is wonderfully improved in health since last year, and is quite a hale old gentleman. He was tenting on the mountains a good part of the time he staid, and was rewarded by finding a new shell, and one or two plants. We went with him an excursion of 3 days, and returned confirmed in the opinion that this Island is the most beautiful spot on the face of the earth."

In 1874 Mr and Mrs Lowe left Liverpool on the *Liberia*, bound for Madeira but the ship did not arrive and was never heard of again.

The Phelps' second son Charlie later married
Reverend Neale's daughter, Agnes.

5 HEALTH

The sanitation system in Madeira at this time left
much to be desired and dysentery was rife, so
various members of the family paid visits to
England for their health. Some of the descriptions
of the treatment given for cholera or dysentery are
interesting if somewhat horrifying!

Dysentery

In July 1847 Anne (often called Kitty), suffered a
severe illness. Elizabeth writes to her husband:
"The whole week has been occupied with mustard
plaisters, hot baths, fomentations, bean poultices, leeches,
and turpentine cataplasms. Thank God! She is so far
better that she has slept quietly today for several hours,
and I am quite in hopes that the worst is past. But she is
still very ill, and never, since last Monday, has swallowed a
morsel of food. She has lived upon iced water and physic,
with sometimes a teaspoon of rice water. Today she has
had a teaspoonful of cold chicken broth which is a great
start. Poor girl! the Carmo festival[8] only finished on
Friday, so that all the time she was at the worst, that
dreadful bell prevented even the chance of a quarter of an
hours forgetfulness. Padre Sá was very kind, and made the

peals as <u>short</u> as possible, but he had no power to remit them. She had no power to sleep however till today, and could not keep quiet a moment, so violent was the irritation.

"It has been a sad week for us all. The violent heat of the weather and the laborious occupation occasioned by an acute disease which has scarcely allowed a moments interval between the preparations and applications, by night and by day, and the bell, and the affliction, altogether have been really hard to bear."

A few days later she continues. "Today there is very little improvement to record. The <u>fever</u> is the most unyielding symptom. Yet she is not delirious, only a little <u>queer</u>. I have been perfectly satisfied with Dr Ross's measures and his attention has been unremitting. He has seen her 3 times a day nearly all the week, and has slept here the last two nights. Some of her symptoms, particularly those that are distinctive of Dysentery, have nearly disappeared, but they are succeeded by others of an anxious kind, and there is every indication of an internal abscess. To add to her misfortunes, she has an external one also, in her face. She has perspired a great deal (Dr Ross's great object) and as of course we are obliged to have the windows open. I think she has caught cold in her glands, and yesterday her ear and throat were so swelled that D^r R thought at first it was the mumps. Today however it appears to indicate a gathering and we have applied 8 leeches in the hope of sending it away. Her beauty will be injured anyway as the leech bites are ugly. She has had leeches twice on her bariga[9] (20 and 16) and last night D^r R bled her in the arm.

"<u>Friday 23 July 4 p.m.</u> Thank God! Our dear child is now really better. She has been carried into Mary's room for the first time today and laid upon the bed. Her face has been very bad and leeched a second time but it is now subsiding, and I think will disperse without breaking. She has had altogether 63 leeches, besides being bled in the arm, but it has been all <u>inevitable</u>. I found Dr Ross very averse to lowering her if it could be avoided."

Almost every member of the family suffered from dysentery at some time and in July 1854, Mary writes to her brother: "We have been very anxious lately about Papa who is just recovering from a most acute attack of dysentery. He had been ailing for some time, but it did not exactly appear what was the matter with him. Last Friday week he went up to Campanario in a broiling sun, as we were spending a few days there, and had to walk a good part of the way as one of his bearers was not very well – the next Sunday he came to town and Dr Lund attended him all the week, but did not think very seriously of his illness till last Saturday when he said it was dysentery, put on leeches and adopted strong measures. That day and the next he was in danger, the inflammation was so very acute, but on Monday he was better and we thought he was all right – but Tuesday he was not so well, and yesterday he came out bright scarlet even to his eyes, as if he had a violent fever.

Dr Lund said he had never seen dysentery take such a turn before, but that it was the crisis of the complaint and would probably carry off the inflammation – and so it was. He passed a good night and looks much more like himself today. He can read a little and take an interest in things, and is only afraid as to eating that he will eat too much."

Cholera

Cholera was an ever present threat and in 1851 one of the letters reports: "I am sorry to say this Steamer brings news that the Cholera is at Grand Canary and very bad. They (this is from the Captain who drank Tea at the Haywards last night) had some Prisoners to land at Canary, and the Governor sent to tell them that the disease was very fatal in the place, that they might put their prisoners ashore at a place he mentioned and he would send a guard of soldiers to meet them, and they would use their own discretion as to having any communication with the shore – which of course they did not. Tenerife will hardly escape. It is nearer to this Island than it has ever been before, and would depopulate it fearfully if it were to come among the Proves. Does Cousin Peyton[10] manufacture Chloride of Lime? If so, it would be a great boon to send out a Cask or two for the Hospital, Prison, and private distribution."

In spite of precautions, a cholera epidemic did sweep through Madeira in 1856 and Mary writes about it to her brother in September.

"I daresay by some means or other you have already learnt of the terrible misfortune that has befallen poor Madeira, and you know that the population is almost decimated by Cholera. Perhaps you are so used to

Cholera in that dreadful country where you live that you don't think much of this, but I assure you it has been an awful time for us and so utterly unexpected that we refused to believe the disease was in the Island till it had been here nearly a month – but it did not show itself in all its virulence till the end of July though the first cases are supposed to have been on the 5th when the troops arrived from Lisbon. Some think they brought it, but I am a non-contagionist, and believe it exists in the atmosphere.

"Two thousand persons have been buried in the two cemeteries of Funchal, being it is said an eighth of the population. In the country it has not in general been so bad, though in one or two parishes the mortality has been even greater as it attacked them unprovided with medicine or medical aid which are very essential weapons in dealing with this monster. In this parish of 2000 about 90 have died, and we consider ourselves to have escaped well. Camacha has suffered about the least as they had two doctors there and 12 resident English families so they had every possible care – a soup kitchen was established at once and cases were attended to immediately. Even so they have lost about 40 (I believe) out of a population of 1600.

"The Haywards have worked very hard here and have had a good deal of sickness in their own house besides. Mrs Hayward has had about 7 little attacks confining her to bed for two or three days each time, and only kept from becoming regular cholera by great care, and George is now regularly laid up with a bad illness which appears to be more dysentery than cholera though I suppose brought on by the disease in the atmosphere. He is quite out of danger and making a good recovery.

"Dr Lund says Mrs Taylor at Camacha has also been very ailing all the summer and Miss Selby has been toiling her life out at the Mount where, though there are many English, she appears to have been the only energetic person. The Stoddarts have been so overburdened with the loss of their youngest daughter Jessie who was the pet and delight of the family, 12 years old.

"Fifteen English have been carried off by this dreadful cholera – Miss Lewis, Mr Edwards, Dr Ross, Mr Gibbs, a baby Broughton and others whose names you do not know. Of course Dr Ross's death was very awful and will make more impression upon people in England than any other. He arrived here from England one Saturday; the following Thursday he was at a merry party of 13 at the Beans - the day after, Friday, he was here on his way down to Town apparently well and talking with great enthusiasm of the new hospital he was establishing in Town and the new method he had adopted for the cure of cholera. That same night Robert was sent for, and Mrs Ross was with him early next morning. At 4 p.m. that day, Saturday, he had ceased to live.

"It was a very mysterious death – the attack was not mysterious because nothing was more natural than that, coming straight from England into an infected region where he took no precautions and exposed himself abundantly to heat and fatigue, neglecting moreover premonitory symptoms for two days, he should be attacked, but the attack was not very severe. He did not get cold nor black, and 2 hours before his death the doctors thought it a promising case. Mrs Ross told us he fell asleep like a tired child.

"We are not the least anxious about ourselves nor have been from the first and we have all been as well as usual. Robert has worked very hard and been to see a good many people in their own houses. We do not believe in contagion – but they won't let me nor anyone but Robert go to the cottages. We here doctored above 400 people and an astonishing number have recovered – considering the utter unskillfulness of their doctors. We are convinced that for ignorant practitioners Brandy and Laudanum are <u>the remedies</u>, followed up with castor oil and assisted at first with rice water and afterwards with beef tea. I trust you may not have much to do with this fearful disease – but if you have, take 20 drops of laudanum with as much brandy as you can stand, repeating and diminishing the dose till you are well. I believe it is almost infallible if taken in time, especially by a teetotaller. Of course it is much worse in India than here, but Major Crone who has lived there all his life has as high an opinion of opium and Brandy as we have. Salt and soda, or emetics, or 100 other things, nitric acid among the number, may be all very well for skilful, scientific men, but they are very little use to amateurs.

"We have been very badly off for doctors. While things were at their worst in Town Dr Juvenal and one or two Portuguese were the only ones the unfortunate people had to depend upon. The consequence was that many died without any medical attendance at all, or had to wait for it till they were nearly dead. The state of the hospital for some days was appalling, but it has wonderfully improved since the first panic and is now particularly well conducted.

"The government has behaved splendidly, and the Portuguese government has really not done amiss – as soon as they heard of our distress in Lisbon they sent a ship with doctors, medicine and food, and from 900 to 1000 persons have been fed at S Francisco ever since, but this supply has almost come to end and there will be great distress when it is discontinued – but it will have saved many valuable lives. The public works were resumed a fortnight ago and many convalescents will have been enabled by it (S Francisco food) to return to them.

"Bella's embroidery trade is a great mercy for the widows and orphans, as she has paid to them nearly 800£ this year for their work. It is very sad how many able bodied men have died. One fancies that they are taken more than any others, but I suppose they are not really, and certainly a great many have recovered. It is delightful when they appear well and smiling to thank us for having cured them. They are most pretty spoken pleasant people and I think we are particularly fortunate in this parish; they are a remarkably nice set.

"We are very sorry for our friends in Campanario, where I spent 3 summers, long enough to get fond of the people there too. They are intensely poor from the want of water in the parish and this year have had no English among them – but the mortality has not been very great in the upper part of the parish which is what we are most acquainted with. In the lower part however they are still dying 6 or 7 a day.

"The English people have been very kind and energetic in sending us drugs and medical comforts to the amount of 300£. They will all be useful I believe and Papa, Robert, Bella and I are all going down tomorrow to be very hard at work distributing them – part are to go to Dr Juvenal and a good deal of rice to Friar Quinta Grande Campanario who is a great friend of ours on account of his devotion to his poor flock who all go into raptures in speaking of him – but the greater part is to go to the English for distribution and of course we reserve the largest portion for ourselves as we flatter ourselves that <u>will</u> be judiciously bestowed. Now I think the disease is <u>quite</u> over in Funchal. The most striking mark of cholera in the Town is the prevalence of mourning, as almost every family has lost a relation."

Tetanus

Other conditions, seldom fatal these days, were also dangerous and in September 1851 Elizabeth says: "The poor Governor and Wife are in great distress, his little boy being dying of a locked Jaw[11] in consequence of a fall. The Portuguese D^{rs} are all squabbling about the treatment. Dr Ross sides with Moderno, but I suppose it doesn't signify."

Yellow Fever

In October 1857 a letter tells of another threat. "The

Yellow Fever is in Lisbon, and also in Tenerife. Humanly speaking it is unlikely that it should come here, but the experience of the Cholera last year has made the inhabitants timorous, and they inflict immense discomfort on all new comers, in the shape of Quarantine. Poor M^r D'Orsey arrived last night, with 4 pupils and a servant, and is imprisoned for 15 days with the rest of the passengers, 48 in all, for only touching at Lisbon, without bringing either mail or passengers from there. We are going to look at him over the wall. The Lazaretto is at the "Louros". Do you remember that place to the east of Funchal? Mrs Gordon and the boys used to go there in the Summer for Sea bathing."

Quarantine

Madeira imposed strict quarantine regulations on arriving passengers if there was any chance they might be bringing an infection. In October 1854 John Crompton was returning to the island after a visit to England. There had been a death on board the ship and after arriving, John writes to his mother: "I wrote a letter to you from the Lazaretto in which we were confined five days. After we had been in some time we got accustomed to it and those who were not very delicate managed to get on tolerably well. We had a large space to walk about in. One evening we got Candido the player on the Machette and Clara Phelps with the rest of the family to come down to the bridge to serenade us."

Home Remedies

Among the many home remedies popular in the 19th Century, Elizabeth recommends the following to her son:

"When the Cholera was so prevalent here, and when we were all feeling the "premonitory" indisposition which, though <u>quite distinct</u>, seems to have some mysterious affinity with Cholera, we were induced, by the evidence of some statistics which came before us, to take <u>Charcoal</u> as a preventative. We all escaped, as you know through the mercy of God, and it would be presumptuous to say that the means He was pleased to put into our hands were inoperative. It agreed so well with me, that I have ever since resorted to it whenever my circulation or digestion seems impaired by heat, fatigue or agitation, as a means of insensibly regulating it. I now make it my request to you that you will take it for a month. It is not disagreeable. It must be freshly burned, and very finely pounded and sifted. The dose is one teaspoonful every other morning mixed with a little sugar and milk, and taken with your breakfast. The swallowing it is far less unpleasant than brushing your teeth with it of which you think nothing."

Tuberculosis

Although all eleven of Elizabeth and Joseph's children survived into old age, their health was far from perfect. Tuberculosis was one of the major causes of death for children and young adults in the 19th century. Even if you survived, the disease could become chronic. Evidence for TB is provided by references to 'psoas abscess' and 'scrofula'.

Psoas Abscess

Elizabeth's concern for Willy's health emerges in her frequent references to 'poor Willy'. He appears to have suffered from convulsions and 'fainting'; however, she first refers to his having a 'psoas abscess' in July 1847 when Willy was 11 years old and at school in England. He would have had TB affecting the discs of his lumbar spine. The infection then tracks down the psoas muscle and produces a lump in the thigh muscle.

"The dear Evanses will have left Bramblebury before you receive this but you (Bella or Fanny) must thank my dear Sister for her note, as I write to nobody but you. Tell her that Dr Ross says Psoas abscess is the same as lumbar abscess and that the only reason he did not use the hard word was because he knew I should not understand it. I still fear that Willy's complaint may run in to that, but the books say that sometimes the tendency to it is overcome when the system can be supported and strengthened. His improvement in appetite is a great object."

In September Elizabeth writes to her husband Joseph strongly urging him to bring Willy home to Madeira before winter for the sake of his health.

"I long much for your next letters, but most of all for those that will tell me you have taken Willy's passage and your own to come out. Mrs Hamond writes that it was already very cold and I cannot bear to think how the poor child's sufferings will be increased by the cold, even during the two months which will probably pass before you do come. I trust nothing will induce you to leave him in England through the Winter, and I am certain dear Anne (Evans) also thinks it would be very bad for him. Moreover the Sea voyage itself is good for him and always agrees with him. Give my best love to him and Arthur."

By the following May things are going better for Willy and Mary writes to her brother Arthur to tell him the good news.

"You will be very glad to hear of Willy being so much better – indeed if it were not for the remains of the swelling in his leg, and his intense aversion to Latin exercises, which surely cannot be natural, he would appear quite well. His great delight is to jump on Jack's back and ride up to the Mount to see the dear Quinta and devour oranges."

However, a year later the tumour persists and Elizabeth writes to Arthur in November 1849:

"His Tumour is not growing larger now, but for some months has been quite stationary. Dr Lund says there is matter in it, but quite in a chronic state and that it is likely there will be no change for years. He has no doubt that it is psoas abscess. Willy seems quite well, and now the weather is cold, often walks up, and still oftener down from here. The two boys still go into the Sea as often as they can."

Two of Willy's sisters, Clara and Janey, also had chronic back problems but it is impossible to tell whether they were suffering from tuberculosis of the spine or scoliosis.

Scrofula

In July 1847 Elizabeth wrote to her sister-in-law, Ann Dickinson, with whom her daughter Fanny was living as a companion, with concerns for the latter's chronic throat problem. This was probably due to scrofula which is tuberculosis of the lymph nodes in the neck.

"In the first place I wish to thank you (and John too) for your parental kindness to Fanny, of which, believe me, I am as sensible as if I told you so by every Packet – in the next, to entreat you to transfer it, for a season, to Bella. I am very uneasy about Fanny's Glands. It is now more than two years that they have been enlarged, and when I reflect that it was <u>cold</u> (at Liverpool) that first deranged them, I feel that it would be wrong to expose her to a third Winter in England without first trying the obvious expedient of removing her to a climate in which she never suffered the least ailment."

Mary, writing to her brother Arthur in April 1858, refers to her sisters' scrofulous tendencies and compares the benign climate in Madeira favourably to the harsher English weather. She is critical of her Dickinson aunt and uncle. Fanny did eventually go out to Madeira later in the same year.

"Bella it is true is but a weakly body – and she <u>probably</u>, one can't be sure, but she probably would have got over the horse's kick better in England than here but she certainly would not have got over her scrofulous tendency in England as rapidly as she has here – in proof of which take Fanny. Both Bella and Fanny were sound till they left Madeira. In England their constitutional tendency was developed in the throats of both of them. Bella returned to Madeira, and in a few months was cured. Fanny staid in England and has been suffering for 11 years. She is not cured yet, and will not be unless people will have the common sense to let her remain here for 18 months, or at least send her out every winter till her tendency is subdued."

Bella sometimes went to Ben Rhydding to take the waters at the spa on Ilkley Moor for health reasons, as mentioned in this letter which she wrote to Arthur in 1858.

"I am now paying visits to friends on my way to Ben Rhydding, where I intend to remain 7 weeks. I wish I had nothing to do after that but to get ready to embark, but unfortunately I have 6 visits to make afterwards which I fear will tire me very much."

Members of the Family who died in Madeira

In the 19th century many British people who suffered from chronic chest complaints, usually tuberculosis, were advised to go to Madeira because of the favourable climate. One of these was George Evans, Elizabeth's nephew. He had contracted TB when he was a medical student at St Bartholomew's Hospital in London and was sent to Madeira to recuperate with his Phelps relations. Sadly he died there on 25 January 1847 and was buried in the British cemetery. In June of that year, Elizabeth writes: "Dear George's Tablet is put up. I shall see it tomorrow."

Then in 1871 John Hubbard, the husband of

Elizabeth's niece Emma, fell ill with a 'chest complaint'. He too travelled to Madeira in the hope of a cure, as did many others, but died shortly afterwards and was interred beside Emma's brother George.

In her letter to Ann Dickinson in 1847 Elizabeth also refers to the many health issues affecting the Phelps family:

"The voice of joy and health has not been heard in our dwelling since this time twelve months when my dear Husband lost his voice. All the winter he was in perpetual danger from the ravages of the Dysentery, and the same disease has just brought my poor Anne into the very jaws of death. Bella's accident has made her lame now for 4 years – Joseph's has disabled him from the profession he was intended to follow – Clara requires much attention from a weakness in her back, and of poor Willy's unaccountable disease, God only knows what will be the event. I may therefore be well excused for a little over anxiety (if it is over) on the ground of health."

Tablets in memory of George Evans and John Hubbard

6 EXPEDITIONS, FIRES AND FLOODS

In 1847 Joseph was in England. Elizabeth spent some of the summer in the mountains and undertook adventurous journeys. In June she writes: "We have all been thinking again and with fresh vigour of the Lombo Grande scheme. I believe we had better take this opportunity of the only Summer in which we are likely to be able to make an exploring party."

It turned out that there was nowhere suitable at Lombo Grande but by July Elizabeth says: "I have hired a Cottage in the Curral das Freiras for 4R to which I was to go early this morning, with Harriet, Anne and Miss Hayward, having sent Joaquim overnight to clean and make preparations." She postponed her departure as Anne was ill, but the others went ahead. "We have sent 7 Mules' loads of chattels 1R each, and have 9 men besides to carry us, so we shall not accomplish our break for nothing. The Lowes are going to pitch their tent (literally) tomorrow near us in Pico Grande till Saturday, and will perhaps return for another week. The Ansfords are coming on Mon 19th and the Rosses on Mon 26th if we stay, and the young men – Haywards, Commodore and Bayman from the Saturdays to Mondays, and we have taken bags to fill with hay for them all to sleep on."

Elizabeth was able to join them when Anne was convalescent and reports that: "It is neither too hot nor too cold and is dry and embracing. I have no doubt K Anne finds it so. The people here are so rich that the respite from beggars is quite delightful. They are however dreadfully unaccommodating. <u>Nothing for nothing</u> is quite the Corral motto. They make it a great favour to <u>sell</u> anything. They are not however, thieves."

By the end of August the news is that "We have had company almost ever since we came, having taken an auxiliary cottage for gents to sleep in. Dr Ross brought over his artist, Mr Simpson, and Mr Mason (who volunteered) on Wed 18, and on Thursday we all went up to Pico Grande and had a glorious day. D^r R returned on Friday, and Mason on Sat^y, on which day Bayman came again, and he and Simpson both left us yesterday. Miss Hayward has been here all the time to meet the artist, who however is far inferior to poor Picken. His object is to take sketches to enable him to paint oil paintings afterwards for sale. He must be back by 1 Oct. He has done a sketch of this cottage for me which is very pretty. Mrs Hope is coming to spend the day tomorrow, so we are quite the fashion.

"We have fixed an excursion for Thursday next (full moon). We are to go all in Hammocks, up the Lombo Grande, and instead of descending into Boa Ventura, turn off to the top of the <u>Ursal</u>, on which is a Chopana[12] built by old Nuno de Freittas for his Pastors[13]. In this we are all to sleep in our hammocks, and proceed next day to the top of P Ruivo, and descend back into the Curral <u>by the near way</u>." **Afterwards she writes**: "The expedition to Pico Ruivo was more successful than any hoick ever was before. Thursday morning arose bright and beautiful and by 12 o'clock were under way. I, Harriet, Clara, Miss Hayward, Methuen and Mason (the two last taking their

horses also up Lombo Grande) in Hammocks, Mr Lowe
on horseback up Lombo Grande intending to walk the
rest of the way, William Hayward walking altogether, and
5 loads. We got to the top of Lombo Grande by 2 and
descançared[14] there a good while examining different
beautiful things and views, and then proceeded, the
greater part of the way on foot, as it was impossible to be
carried over such places, to the "Chopana do Ursal"
which we reached by 5 o'clock. Oh! How I did long for
you to see that glorious sight: a sea of cloud filling the
Boa Ventura and every ravine, and the noble crests
standing out of it. This is the most beautiful place that
ever was seen. A large flat, as large as the Penfold's
Achada, covered with Heath Trees, and a nice fountain of
water, the temperature of which was 42°F. We passed the
night <u>very</u> comfortably, all on dry Ursa[15], which is a most
luxurious bed.

"We got up to see the Sun rise, and found the sea of
clouds all cleared away and the clearness so great that
every distant object seemed perfectly distinct. It was the
most beautiful sight I had <u>then</u> seen. We overlook all the
N and W parts of the Island from <u>that</u> point, and it was
such a pleasure to me and Mr Lowe to trace our former
wanderings down the road from the Estanquinhos to S
Vicente. After breakfast we struck our tent, and sent it
and the greater part of our luggage, blankets etc back and
proceeded to P Ruivo. We had to retrace our steps part of
the way, and then proceed Eastward. The hammocks were
of very little use, the <u>staircase</u> being too irregular to admit
them. The only thing in favour of it is that there are in

general balusters, the brush wood being so thick that you have to force your way through. I kept wondering whether you would have miolo[16] to get over such places. I did not mind the precipices at all, but was wholly unable to master the ascent without help, so was forced to be dragged up by a savage. Oh! the glory of the 3 phenomena we witnessed – the setting of the sun, the rising of the Harvest moon (on the second night of her fullness) and the rising of the sun. I shall never be happy till I have been there with you. However the question is now fully set at rest, whether you see the Sea all round – you do, with the exception of two little peaks of Pico da Torre which rise above the horizon thus. Do ascertain from your philosophical friends whether this positively implies that these two peaks are absolutely higher than the point of view, or whether their distance from this has anything to do with the question. Over the Paul, Pico Grande and the whole circle with this exception, you see it (the horizon) and no mistake.

"We started downwards soon after Sunrise, and breakfasted at the first fountain, then reached home about 4 hours later. After a good dinner and abundant ablutions (most of the party resorting to the river) we were all quite fresh."

Late in September Elizabeth tells of another expedition. "We have been another awful climb up the mountains. It was last Friday when I, Harriet, Clara, Annette McKellar, Commodore and Charles Hayward set off up Cedrão. We were accompanied by the only man in this parish who knows all the passes of it, being a

Goatherd who shares it with Pedro Agastinho's tenants, who are S Antonio men. We took 3 hammocks which had nearly a sinecure, but not so their bearers who had to drag us up most wonderful places. The passes are much worse than those of P Ruivo, but as we all had "miolo" it didn't signify and we finally accomplished getting up to the Chopana by 2 o'clock. But here, as before on P Ruivo, I struck. To get down those places in the same day I felt to be impossible, so we ate our dinner and sent down a savage for Tea and blankets. We were very fortunate in finding the S Antonio Shepherds on the spot, who having already killed a goat, sold us some of it for the men and lent us their kettle to boil it.

"So all fared well and were in good humour, but the elements were not so propitious as on former occasions, and a thick mist came on which shut out all the peaks one after the other from our view. But even this was a beautiful process and we enjoyed it much. The S Antonio men now departed, but gave such an inviting account of the passage from there to the Arreiros, that two of the party, Harriet and Commodore, determined to take that route and go into Town by it the next morning so they detained one out of the three S Antonio men to shew them the way. In the mean time, night drew on and the servant returned from the Corral with our supper having been just 4 hours absent! The ascent alone had cost us nearly 6 with all our dragging.

"We prepared our bed as on former occasions with heather, but did not fare so well as the Chopana was full of fleas from the dogs having slept there. We turned out before day to see not the glorious sunrise, but wonderful clouds obscuring it. It was a real Scotch Mist but did not deter H and William Hayward from their adventure, and we parted after breakfast. Our descent being immediate, we were soon in sunshine, but they were in cloud for about an hour which they found an advantage, as they did not want to be dazzled. The places they went over were frightful, though perfectly safe and easy in point of fact – it is only in imagination that walking over a dyke 18 inches wide with a precipice on each side is terrible. However they thought it necessary to tie ropes round H's waist, which she voted quite superfluous.

"This was my last excursion and I have derived as much benefit as pleasure from them. It was quite touching to hear the savages wishing that the meninas[17] of their amo[18] (T Agostinho) would do the same."

In 1851 Joseph took his third daughter Anne (Kitty) to England to be married to Robert Bayman, another Madeira wine merchant who was also the American vice-consul there. When the newly-weds returned to Madeira, Joseph stayed on in England to try to obtain orders for his wine. While he was away Elizabeth and her youngest daughter Jane spent some time with the Rev and Mrs Lowe in the Curral das Freiras. She writes news of a dreadful fire. "It is, as you know, a great pleasure to me to be domiciliated with Lowe, and a treat to look upon the mountains. The pleasure of my visit has however been not damped, but frustrated by a public misfortune, a Fire in the Serra, which for magnitude and duration exceeds anything that has occurred in our time, and will nearly put the finishing stroke to the physical prosperity of this unfortunate Island. We are (humbly be it spoken) safe here, because Cedrão is a bare rock that could not conduct the Fire, and the Villões have means to prevent its walking down the Valley, but we are in sight of it in 4 different directions and its blazing last night was so frightful that we could not cease looking at it till near 1 o'clock when it died away a little. It was burning beautiful Louro Trees to which we had been walking very near on the same afternoon, and was providentially stopped by a Corgo from spreading into the largest forest in the Serras of the Corral (Rainha[19] Marita) which extends all up the side of the Lombo Grande to the Boeadas Torrinhas, the Trees of which though not burned are so singed by the heat, that today they look all brown though yesterday they were beautifully green. Lombo Grande is all burned; so is the beautiful Feijao da Coita; so is (we hear) the Boaventura. The Fire is however extinguished or about to be so, in all these places, but on the Paul there is no chance or possibility of its being put out till the Winter rains come. So also in all the <u>heights</u> and <u>Mountains</u>, where no <u>attempts</u> even can be made to check it, on account of the inaccessibility of the rocks. The source of this river, the most abundant in the Soretta, will therefore be denuded of Trees and dried up, and instead of the abundant stream in which Janey and I bathed this morning, in a few years there will be a dry bed and no corn, wine and <u>beans</u> in this parish. Nor is this all. Funchal will be greatly affected by the diminution of the Levada dos Piornais.

"I returned on Saturday with Lowe and thought it my duty to go to José Silvestre, and tell him what we had seen in the Serra, and the laziness or indifference of the local authorities. He seemed much obliged but rather perplexed what to do, as it ought to rest with the Camara. La se avenha[20]!"

Another of Elizabeth's letters tells of a visit she paid to a wealthy local family.

"On Wed 1 Oct we went on to the Leals, in company with Miss Aranjo, who was also going to stay. What a beautiful place, and what kind people! They received me as if I had been their dearest friend, and entertained us for a week like a queen. What good living! The Portuguese seem to me to beat the English hollow at eating and drinking, for they had as much on the table in one day as we have in a week. Such roasts, boils and stews! Such Turkeys, Ducks and Chickens! Such pickles, olives and periwinkles! Such cream cheeses, almond puddings and doces[21]! Such Peaches, Nectarines and Pineapples! And all eaten with so many Silver handled knives, Urns and Salvers that I was astonished at the appearance of wealth and plenty in that remote locality. The family consists of (1) old D Gertrudes who has been stone blind for 7 years but who is cheerful and unfeignedly religious, and (2) her "company keeper" D Thomasia, sister of Candido Velloza, (3 and 4) Valentini and his wife, (5.6.7) their 3 boys Adolfo aged 15, João aged 14 and Alfredo 12, and (8) Mr João Leal, Valentini's brother. But I did not see this last as he was at S Anna receiving the Wines there. Also Valentini was living at the house on the Beach as it was the thick of the Vintage so I only saw him twice, once when we went down to visit him (further than from the Mount to Funchal) and on Sunday when he spent the day at the Quinta.

"The boys are very nice. They speak English very well, having learned of Miss Cane, but I suppose had only read English as a task, and Portuguese books are not entertaining so that their delight when I read to them a really interesting tale (The Steadfast Gabriel by Miss M Howitt) was beyond anything you can imagine. They were so sorry when we came away. They are very well disposed boys, and I do not feel at all afraid of them as companions for Willy as I saw nothing to disapprove of in their bringing up. They are not worked as hard as they might be with advantage, and I should fear Mr Williams's was not the best school in the world for them.

"We walked all about that beautiful parish, and I thought of the time when we were there together. The Leals seem to manage their estates very well and to do a great deal of good – the Proves[22] coming to them for physic and food just as they do to us, so that sometimes D Augusta was employed for several hours in attending to them. She and I interchange most affectionate notes since I am come back."

Floods were also a regular feature of Madeira, and still occur to this day, the steep terrain allowing them to do great damage. In 1856 a letter from Fanny to Arthur tells of one: "There has been a flood in Madeira – on the 5th Jan it happened. It has not done so much damage as usual, but it has carried off all the

Yams grounds, on which the poor people depended for their summer subsistence, and I am afraid there will be a great deal of famine and trouble and of course our people will give away a great deal more money than they can well afford which is a bore, and hardly right besides."

As a result of fires, droughts and floods, Madeira had become denuded of trees. Elizabeth Phelps realised that trees were essential to the well-being of the islanders, and often sent to England for suitable trees, seedlings and seeds, which were planted all over their estates. She frequently organised large picnic parties and each of the guests would be given a seedling tree, and required to plant it at the spot before leaving. Frances Roper, born Hubbard, a great granddaughter of Elizabeth Phelps's sister Anne Evans, visited Madeira in 1954 and she discovered that in after years these clumps of trees had grown and flourished, and to within living memory were always known as "Mrs Phelps's Picnic Places."

Curral das Freiras: Lithograph by Andrew Picken 1840

7 FOREIGN VISITORS

Many English families spent the winters in Madeira, though not many made it their permanent home. Ships from European ports bound for South America, South Africa or the Orient often called at Madeira so transport was abundantly available, though some of the journeys were extremely uncomfortable. This letter tells of one voyage in February 1858 which, one hopes, was the exception rather than the rule!

"We only landed yesterday morning – and after such a passage. I hope some other line of packets may be invented, for if the *Armenian* is the best of the Africans, it is a wonder that anybody reaches anywhere alive. Captain Corbett was very kind to people but he couldn't mend his ship. We started about four on Sunday afternoon, and made a false start to begin with, and had to go back and begin again. Then when we got out of Plymouth Harbour we found ourselves in a tremendous sea. The ship was so badly laden with the wrong things at the top that she rolled dreadfully. Captain Corbett said if there had been any wind besides we should have been in a bad way. On Monday afternoon when we were in the chops of the Channel we had to lay to for 24 hours which was so sickening.

"Poor we were in the Ladies cabin, a very tiny one with four berths. We luckily had the two top ones at right angles to each other. Under me was a Mrs Leggatt with a little boy 3 years old. Under Kate was intended to be M^rs

John Payn and infant two months old, but she found it close so she and the baby and her Portuguese maid, and a bassinette and a quantity of luggage were on the floor the whole voyage – so that Kate and I had to have every individual thing on our own berth – and as the sailors had no time to take the heavy luggage down below until Wednesday morning and there was no tarpaulin put over it until the middle of Sunday night we were rather in a state of mind feeling certain that it must be spoiled. However the things are just come and all is quite right, not touched at all by the wet.

"We were very sick until Wednesday morning, I worse than ever before, in that wretched cabin, but after that the weather was fair and we were on deck every day from ten in the morning until ten at night. Of course it was impossible to wash or dress under the circumstances, and we never took off our clothes the whole time, and the African Company was not liberal enough to allow of any moveable hand-basins; there was but one in the Cabin and that a fixture. I never could have believed in such authorized discomfort, in spite of the kindness of all officials on board.

"On Wednesday night Mrs Leggatt's husband, one of a lot of Officers going to Sierra Leone, was taken with delirium tremens – and the first manifestation of it took place in our cabin. He put his finger on Kate's mouth, and told her some mysterious secret. He was very bad indeed, and for several hours was not expected to live. Luckily there was a passenger D^r on board who brought him through. We want to know how many passengers the

Act of Parliament requires for a surgeon for there was great use for one. An arm was broken in the Gale and 3 stewards were washed away. They were washed back again but it made them very ill, and they wanted looking after and couldn't do much for us at first. I believe we should have died of the screams of Mrs Payn's ill-managed baby, but for a goodnatured mulatto woman, who looked after us; the Steward took very little heed of us. Mrs Leggatt had to go and nurse her husband two nights and Kate and I each took her child for one. He was a very nice one and very fond of us, but it was rather a tight fit in our berths. We were so thankful when the man got better for it was such a bore to expect quarantine on our arrival which I suppose was inevitable if he had died.

"We were off the Island at two on Sunday morning and weighed anchor, but didn't approach until 6 o'clock, so we were up on deck and had a glorious view of the Mountains with the first snow on them we had seen this Winter, and the Sunrise."

Many aristocratic visitors and even royalty came from Europe to Madeira and local residents were keen to secure their patronage. In June 1847, Elizabeth writes to her husband:

"The Queen Dowager[23] and the King of Holland[24] have both applied indirectly for the Augustias, that is Mrs Knox has written to Mrs Gordon to inquire of D^r McKellar if he still wishes to let it, she having been sent for by the Princess Sophia to give her all particulars of Madeira but she does not say she is authorised to take it. Mr Montino the Dutch Consul has enquired if it will be disengaged for his King. Now the probability is that the

Queen will eventually go to M[r] Stoddart's 2 houses Town and Country, and the King to Count Carvalhal's, and D[r] McKellar be left in the lurch. The Countess Egloffstein[25] would be a better tenant than either, as she will perhaps stay some years, and I have promised D[r] McK that M[rs] Evans will recommend it to her.

"M[r] Hasche has taken half the *Eclipse* for the Countess in Sept (she is going into Dock till then) so he is in communication with her and I fear may have it in contemplation to let old Baccalhaō's large new house in the Hortas to her, but the Augustias is a much better situation. Above all, engage her to come <u>here</u> on landing, else she will never do us any good, nor we her.

"I did think of recommending D[r] M[c]Kellar's house to the Queen Dowager, but I did not think of recommending your Wine. Bayman however observes that you are the only Merchant who has any right to her Majesty's orders, from the Evans's acquaintance with Lord Howe, who, as Comptroller of the Household, or Lord Chamberlain, or something, has probably the uncontrolled power to choose. If once Her Majesty tastes the Consul's Wine, the chance for bringing Madeira wine into fashion and repute is lost. I wish that you could obtain an order for sending a small supply into her house before she comes. If once she tasted your wine, her orders would be certain. I do not think it is too much to ask of Lord Howe to do this. The household ought certainly to have the privilege of choosing between or among the different Merchants by having a specimen of their different Wines put before them. I would however rather that W Gordon had her orders than anybody else except ourselves, as it is important that he should taste good Wine.

"Wed 30 June. Mrs Hope has had a letter from Mrs Forbes, full of the Queen Dowager who seems likely to take the Augustias. You must all exert yourselves to try and get our fair share of advantage out of the Royal visit. I think Mrs Grover was very intimate with Lady Howe as Miss Gore. Is she coming out? But above all you must propitiate Countess Egloffstein and engage her to come to the house on landing. We can surely entertain her better than Mrs Hasche can. Leave no stone unturned I entreat. Has Bella written an essay for either as she did for the Duchess of Manchester?"

Frances Roper was one of the unpaid young ladies who worked in Aunt Janey's Orphanage for a time and she records: "The Phelpses must have been the leading English family in Madeira at that period, as it fell to them to entertain all the visiting Royalties and notabilities. During the last years of her life, Aunt Janey, who was then close on eighty years of age, told me that she remembered as a small child being brought down to the dining room after dinner, and sitting upon the knee of the Emperor Napoleon III, [as he later became] and being fed by him with fruit and nuts."

Another royal visitor was the Empress of Brazil who came to Madeira with her daughter in November 1852. One of the letters to Arthur at this time asks:

"Have you heard of the great fact that we are so proud and pleased at? namely that the Empress of Brazil who is now here for the benefit of her daughter's health has sent to request Mary to be her almoner. Mary was so delighted for she knows such numbers of starving people. The D^r of the princess came to speak to Mary about it and told her that her Majesty having heard of Mary's kindness to the poor and being dissatisfied with the way in which her money was given by the priests, begged she would distribute some for her. Mary having accepted this office, the D^r the next day brought down £25 and said she was to receive the same every month. M spent this money in about a fortnight and sent in some account of the way it had been spent; and a few days after down came £10 more so that she has already had £35 and been less than a month at it. We heard afterwards that the Empress had expressed herself as highly satisfied with the way Mary had acquitted herself. It is very pleasant though it takes poor Mary about 2 or 3 hours every day."

The Princess Maria Amélia died of tuberculosis in Funchal in February 1853 and the Empress decided to build a hospital there in memory of her daughter. She appointed Joseph Phelps as Treasurer of this undertaking. In September 1859, Elizabeth writes:

"Papa is often in Town – on the affairs of the Hospicio building by the Empress Dowager of Brazil, for consumption. Of course some of us have told you long ago, that H M appointed him Treasurer – a nomination highly honourable to him, tho' not particularly so to the nation for whom the charity is founded. We are, as you know, preparing for a visit of some duration to England. But the delays in completing the Empress's Hospital will

51

probably make it late in the Summer before we go, as the Papa w⁴ not think it right to throw up his office before it naturally expires."

The Hospício da Princesa Dona Maria Amélia eventually opened in 1862. The Archduke Maximillian of Mexico, to whom the princess had been betrothed, financed two wards until his death. Many educated and talented people from Europe came to visit Madeira. Mary writes to Arthur in 1856:

"Harriet has "sat" twice to Mʳˢ Murray a fine artist who out of pure philanthropy offered to do her and will I am sure make a very pretty picture. She is doing Arthur Bayman and the Forbses for pay and I believe her terms are high. She is also here only for a short time on her way from Tenerife where her husband is Consul, to England where she is going for her health and has an immense deal to do, so it is excessively kind of her to take all this gratis trouble for us. I like her very much. Did you ever hear of Heaphy[26] her father? She says he was a famous water colourer.

"We have had a very quiet winter except for the two floods, and if there had been balls without end I should not know what to say to you about them. We go often to tea with "Donkin of Oxford"[27] who plays very well – nothing to compare to Mʳ Lowe tho'. Clara learns singing very diligently of Mʳ Rakemann who hopes to make something of her. He is a capital musician and Master."

And in 1859, Janey writes that

"Such numbers of people are coming out this winter that almost all the houses are taken besides rooms in the

boarding houses. A large Steamer the *'Clyde'* is bringing
lots of families who were here last year, Forbses andc."

8 MUSIC AND CONCERTS

Music played a large part in the Phelps's lives.
Most of the family played an instrument –
pianoforte, harp, a local guitar called a machete, or
the organ. Musical parties were given regularly.
The following excerpts from letters give an idea of
the musical life in Madeira at the time.
In 1847 "The Lowes and Goodban[28] and Agastinho
coming to play, and I have invited M[rs] Hope and Bayman
– nobody else. Kitty Anne plays her Trio beautifully and
has rehearsed it once with Goodban.

"I am in hopes of selling Lowe's Piano through
Candido[29]. I am quite ashamed of the time Candido and
Cabral have spent upon Harriet and Clara. Should they
not be paid somehow? Clara's Machete has obtained
unbounded applause from the Corral up to the top of
Pico Ruivo."

In January 1852 "There have been some very nice
parties this year, but as you are not fond of dancing you
do not miss them. M[r] Lowe played a great deal of music
last night to a highly delighted audience as also Candido
and Cabral on the Machete and Guitar."

In April 1853 "There is a professor of music here
just now. I never heard any one play so magnificently. He
is coming to tea tonight which he has done sometimes

before and which is very pleasant. His name is Pfeiffer and he is the son of that Mme Ida Pfeiffer who went round the world. He is a gentlemanly person and is on his way to Brazil."

From Harriet to Arthur in February 1854 "I like the organ book you sent me very much. I wanted something of the sort and think it may do me good as my organ playing is by no means artistic. I very seldom play on our home organ and there is only church on Wednesday and Friday besides Sunday so that there is not much practising for me. Mary generally plays though I take my turn sometimes but I prefer singing.

"How very nicely Clara sings - and what a pretty selection of songs she has. I must rub up my singing which I had quite left off that I may sing duets with her. If ever you have time from your numerous avocations, you must take lessons especially in singing at sight which is the nicest thing possible when one can do it. And then ten years hence! You and I may perhaps sing together."

In April 1856 "We were at a grand dinner party the other night given to the American ambassadors, O'Sullivans, who however were not there - only her sister, Miss Rogers, one of the most favourable specimens of a Yankee young lady I ever saw. Kitty seemed tired and did not entertain her guests with much spirit, so this task principally fell to Harriet and Clara, who performed with their voices and on the guitar and Machete, without however, I thought, eliciting the admiration they deserved."

In August 1856 from Clara to Arthur "We have

the German Professor Mr Rakemann staying with us this Summer, on a mutual accommodation principle. We keep him and feed him and he teaches Mary and me music. He does play delightfully and is a first rate Master. I sing away in fine style, and am supposed to have improved wonderfully under his experienced tuition. Are you better off for Music at Bombay than you were at that horrid other place?"

In February 1859 "I wish you could be present at some of our concerts, they are so delightful. I wonder if your voice is as good as Joe's. We are preparing for our last concert tomorrow before he goes.

"28th Our concert was most successful. There were 78 people present, and we performed 20 pieces of music. We are so delighted at your being able to train a choir – and wish we could hear you sing. It is charming the Phelps musical tastes breaking out spontaneously in you."

Joseph to Arthur in September 1860 "We are all comfortably settled in dear Aunt Fanny's house in Young Street, and she does all in her power to make us happy. We have got a piano, and last Tuesday we had some friends to dine with us, among others Clara and her husband. She played the Machettinho de Braga exquisitely; I never heard her play better."

Joseph to Elizabeth in 1862, when he had returned to Madeira to pack up. "We had a brilliant party of about 50 - Mrs Hinton and M^{rs} R Wilson, the Selbys, Haywards, Basão de Paive, the Hon Misses Edwardes etc etc. Lowe and Mr Donkin played a duet (Pianoforte and Fiddle). Anne played the Serenade with

Lowe beautifully, and an American amateur said he was astonished to hear music so beautifully executed. Mrs Donkin and Julia sang. M^{rs} and Miss Ogle were of the party, Charles Coneybeare and his pupil Knatchbull. We had a beautiful spread in the large dining room a la Carmo! We are to have two more parties Thursday and Saturday before Lowe goes to the Westward."

A machete de braça dating to 1846 such as Clara Phelps would have played

9 SCHOOL AND VISITING TUTORS

Although Joseph's reason for being in Madeira was to manage the family wine-making and export business, he and Elizabeth became very involved with the local community and each started a school, for local boys and girls respectively, where reading, writing and practical skills were taught. Many educated people and even royalty from Europe came to spend the winter in Madeira. These visitors were encouraged to contribute funds for the schools.

In a letter of October 1851, Elizabeth describes how "Mr Davies has done me a <u>disfeita</u>[30] that I cannot get over at all. It is in the person of the School. He has cut off the Mistress from the little bit of yard or garden, by building up a Wall straight off from the corner of the house to the entrance door – and this is in spite of my urgent remonstrance and entreaty by letter. He took the opportunity when D^r O was absent at S George for 2 days, he (the D^r) having declared that it should not be done. James (Sheffield) says we must take it as a warning to quit, and so I would gladly, if I could find any other place that would suit us, but J Silvestre has given me a list of the Fazenda[31] houses and we can't find one that would do."

Some solution must have been found, however, as in April 1853, Elizabeth writes to her son: "The pleasantest episode that has occurred in our life of late, has been the visit of the Empress of Brazil to the Girls' School. Your Sisters and I (with the other members of the School Society) received H. M., and she talked with us for 2½ hours and examined every detail of the School with a most scrutinizing exactness. She is a good judge, and I am happy to say gave it her most unqualified approbation, saying she was so convinced that the System[32] pursued was the best possible, that she should endeavour to introduce it in Lisbon. I am sorry to say that she is going next month, and has finished the charity she dispensed thro' Mary. She gave £25 to the School."

Visitors to Madeira sometimes conducted small temporary English colleges. One such was Mr D'Orsey, a Scottish clergyman. A letter of June 1851 says: "D'Orsey is well in health apparently, but his lungs are diseased and Dr Ross says he must not pass next Winter in Glasgow so he is thinking of bringing out M^{rs} D'Orsey, and if he does, and another pupil or two, I hope we may be able to place Willy with him as a boarder."

Mr D'Orsey's school operated for some years during the winter months, and in October 1852, Harriet writes to her brother: "We very often go in and see the School and it is so very amusing. There are nearly 20 boys already attending it regularly and several more expected who have not come in from the country, so that he (M^r D) is in a thriving way."

In August 1853 the news is that "M^r D'Orsey is in Lisbon. He is coming back with M^{rs} D and all the family next month, to open the College again on the 1 Oct."

In July 1854 Mary writes to her brother Arthur who had recently begun his Army career in India: "Recommend the Madeira Collegiate if you have an opportunity. I suppose a case might occur of children in India requiring a climate between India and England. The terms for boarders are about 100£ according to age – about 20£ for day pupils. It is wonderfully good teaching and as kind and conscientious a master as you could find."

Many other visitors gave less formal classes to small groups, in music, art or languages and the Phelps daughters managed to learn German, Latin and even Greek from visiting tutors. Clara met her future husband when he came to Madeira as tutor to an English family. (The Phelps's four sons were all sent to England for their education, to a school run by their uncle in Leicestershire.)

10 OTHER FAMILY OCCUPATIONS AND EVERYDAY LIFE

When not busy with the affairs already described under the various headings above, members of the family found time for other hobbies or entertainments, some of which are mentioned in the letters. In November 1849, Elizabeth writes to Arthur at school in England:

"I will tell you a little how we are disposed of at present. Harriet and I are taking care of Janey and Helen Langford, who is a very sweet little girl, and the two are very happy together. Arsenia also, the Feitor's[33] daughter, is allowed to play with them and they are at present very intent upon skipping, which not one of them can do, and their awkwardness is very amusing.

"The lessons too, go on with more spirit with a second little girl to enliven them, and Helen has a wonderful talent for mental arithmetic, in which Janey is not deficient, nor Willy either, and we all form a grand class of <u>counting</u>, every evening. This would be famous amusement for you boys, and help you on with your sums beyond what you can believe. It consists in counting forwards and backwards as far as 100 (or more) – not only one by one, but two by two, etc, as far as 20 by 20. If you examine these figures (I mean in all the numbers) you will find they possess many curious properties and progressions." **In 1850 Mary writes**:

"Papa and Mama spent the day at the Allegria yesterday spearing eels with the Matthewses and Peacockes (who are our neighbours at S Roque) but I have not heard whether they had good sport, as Mama is not yet come down and Papa is gone to breakfast on board the *Brilliant*."

In May 1851 Charlie writes:

"I have been up every night this week at parties till past midnight; on Wednesday I went to the Taylors and I got up the next morning at 5 o'clock and walked to Camacha[34] where I arrived before 7. It was a nice cool day though very hot in town. I walked all over the place shooting with a Portuguese man and we got 14 Blackbirds. I came down to town before 5 o'clock, copied some letters and afterwards went to the Rosses where I enjoyed myself dancing and playing Busca Tres[35], and went to bed at past 11. Why don't you play at Busca Tres in England; it is such capital fun and so easy to learn."

Among the other English families who made their home in Madeira were the Blandys, whose wine business still flourishes today. There had been coolness between the families as they had taken opposite sides on the controversy about Rev Lowe.

Elizabeth writes to her husband in August 1851:

"I have induced Mary to accept an invitation from Mrs Charles Blandy (M^r C B being in England) and she spent last week at Campanario with her accordingly. She (M) says their household is very well conducted, and their children very well brought up. She had not much enjoyment of the country at Campanario on account of the leste[36] and the Fires which were as frightful there as at the Corral. It was at the same time that I was at the latter and I find the lights were then visible from Town."

And in September she says: "I am glad Mary <u>did</u> go and stay with the Charles Blandys. I didn't know they were about to leave the Island, but would rather that they should not depart with the impression that we had been uncivil." **Always ready to promote local industry, Elizabeth must have procured a wicker cot for a friend. She tells Joseph:** "Mrs Caldbeck writes me a very civil note of thanks for helping Captain C to get a Bassinette. I am sorry not to see the Captain this trip, but pray tell him I heartily wish him joy of his wife's recovery."

In August 1853 a new craze reached Madeira.

"We are great believers in Table turning here, and our faith is not shaken by Professor Faraday's ingenious "tests". It seems quite possible that the involuntary muscular action of which he speaks may be a necessary concomitant or channel for the "od force", but that the latter may nevertheless be real. And this seems the more probable because those persons who have least of the first, have sometimes most of the last, as Mrs Plowden. It is impossible to witness the almost instantaneous effect which her hands have on the table without believing that it is something distinct from pushing. Did you ever see her try?" **One of Arthur's sisters tells him in May 1858**: "We are at present very busy entertaining Danes or being entertained by them. We dined with them at the Selbys on Tuesday and tonight we expect them here to dance. It is the first dance we have given Fanny so I hope it will be a success. We have only had 9 concerts <u>here</u>, but altogether she has had no lack of gaiety. The Danes are always pleasant, with their travels in Ireland and reminiscences of the King's visit here.

"The great occupation of the Phelpses lately has been bathing in the sea. Clara has become a proficient in swimming and Fanny and Janey are gradually acquiring the art. They go in a boat to Mr Grant's house in the Pontinha the garden of which as perhaps you may remember opens onto the sea, and there enjoy themselves. It has done them an immense deal of good, especially Mama and Janey."

Janey took up photography with great enthusiasm and in 1859 Elizabeth writes

"The child is at this time absolutely absorbed in Photography. Mr Hinton has lent her a Camera, and Russell Gordon has most goodnaturedly furnished her with books, and taken great pains in instructing her, and I have allowed her time, and all facilities for practice, to the great detriment of hands, dresses and towels. But it is an immensely difficult art, and requires much exactness of manipulation – so that her success has not yet been complete. Her perseverance however is indomitable, so she will be sure to succeed at last. She is now printing a faint image of your respected parents to enclose in this.

"Janey's whole soul is just now absorbed in Photography – divided with "Croquet" or "lawn billiards" a game of balls struck with mallets, which I need not describe, but which has infected all the male and female, English and Portuguese, adult and juvenile gentry of Madeira with a general fury this summer. The Gordons and Stoddarts have advantageous fields for it here, and at Camacha there is turf everywhere, so that Janey often has a good game, and has extemporized a humble imitation at home. This is far more in her way than letter writing and is better for her health." **Janey says:**"People are very hard at work with archery now and a game called Croquet played on the grass with balls, hoops stuck in the ground and a bell."

Elizabeth Phelps and her 3 sisters. She is 2nd from the left and Anne Evans on the far right.

11. LATER LIVES OF THE FAMILY

Joseph and Elizabeth Phelps moved to England in 1860, though Joseph returned to pack up and hand over Carmo house to their daughter Kitty and her husband Robert Bayman who remained there for some years. They bought 64 Larkhall Rise, Clapham, naming the house 'Carmo'. There they led busy lives for some years, seeing grandchildren from Natal, Newfoundland or India, as well as friends and relatives in England. They both died at this house, 11 days apart, in April 1876. Mary writes to her brother Arthur in Bombay to tell him about it: "My dearest Arthur, I have such sorrowful news for you, that it is difficult to write it. Your happy anticipations of welcome home to your parents all come to an end. It is so sudden & so sad – you are so entirely unprepared. You were not perhaps altogether unprepared to hear of Papa's death but that Mama, full of life & energy as she was, should go too we none of us expected."

Their 11 children's lives are summarised below. Arthur, having gone to India straight from school in England at the tender age of 16, told his mother that he felt he did not know his sisters. She wrote a long and very objective reply from which we were able to learn much valuable information. Some of Elizabeth's comments on her daughters as well as excerpts from Frances Roper's writings, are given below.

1 Bella Born in Madeira 25 October 1820.

Her mother says, "Bella has perhaps the most powerful mind of any of them. She grasps a subject in all its bearings with a ready comprehensiveness, and retains it with the tenacity of a particularly retentive memory. She has read more than most women (or men) and her mind is therefore well stored. But she has suffered a good deal in body. You remember how she was kicked by a horse in the leg, 15 years ago. Well, the leg has been comparatively powerless ever since. There never was any wound; and the bruise passed off as other bruises do, but the Tendon was severed, and (as Sir Chas Clarke immediately informed us) never could unite again, it being the nature of tendons to <u>retract</u> and keep their points distant when severed. So she has been greatly deprived of exercise, and this has acted unfavourably upon her general health. The only way by which she can keep herself in any condition for work, mental or bodily, is by taking the weight of her body off her limbs for a regular portion of the day, in addition to her natural rest by night. She therefore retires to her own apartment every afternoon to maintain the horizontal position for the space of 2 hours, and the rigidity with which she enforces this rule upon herself constantly draws upon her the accusation of being "selfish, "unaccommodating", "indolent" etc but she perseveres, believing it to be her duty to preserve whatever portion is granted to her of the precious talent of health by the means which she <u>knows</u> from experience to be essential to that end.

"I think she has felt it rather a hardship to be blamed for her infirmities and has perhaps rather deteriorated in the points of warmth or affection in her disposition generally, though towards the many friends who have understood this, she is attached and affectionate. Her piety is deep and sincere, and so far influences her life as to keep under control a temper naturally hasty. She leads a very laborious life, never shrinking from any (mental) exertion by which she can serve herself or others." Elizabeth then describes her work with the embroidery which has been quoted under that heading.

After moving to England with her parents in 1860, Bella lived with them at the house in Clapham, though she often visited other relations or spent time in East Grinstead as she was an Associate of the Society of St Margaret, established in 1854 by Dr Neale. She lived at the Carmo, Clapham with her sister Mary, until her death in 1893, aged 78.

2 Mary   Born in Madeira 4 August 1822.

As a young child Mary lived with her uncle and aunt (Arthur and Anne Evans) at Market Bosworth in England for a time, for health reasons; though in later life she had good health. Like the other daughters, she did not have formal schooling but was educated by her mother, aunt and visiting tutors and by wide reading. She was responsible for teaching her young brothers before they went to England.

Her mother's account is: "If ever a high degree of the saintly character has been attained to in the 19th Century, it is in the person of your sister Mary. She has so effectually given up her whole soul to the law of Christ that every thought seems to be brought into captivity to it. By their fruits ye shall know them. It is only by observing the total renunciation of self, the active benevolence, the uncompromising practice of duty, that you are aware of the power of religion in her heart, for you never hear of it. But she is a blessing to the whole household. She too, has an uncommon capacity, but cultivates it less than she otherwise would do from her habit of giving up her own pursuits and her own time, to the claims of others. She did however find time only two years ago, to study Latin with M^r D'Orsey, and had attained to a thorough understanding of and enjoyment of Virgil when our departure into the country interrupted the lessons, and before they could be resumed, Janey came out (to Madeira), and occupied the limited space of the day which either she or M^r D'Orsey could devote to separate study, so perhaps she may never take her degree, but M^r D'O says she is now better acquainted with the language than most undergraduates.

"We have it not in our power to give a great deal of Money to the poor, but Mary makes amends for limited donations by her powerful assistance in directing and advising them. She is acquainted with almost all the poor, and with their particular circumstances and assists one to rebuild their cottage, and another to obtain employment, one to buy seed for planting, another flax for spinning, intercedes with the landlord for this one and with the Doctor for that one. Anybody who wishes to benefit the poor, naturally applies to her to know how to do it, so that she often receives assistance which enables her to extend her benefits to a far greater amount than we could do ourselves. When the Empress of Brazil was here in 1853 she appointed Mary her almoner for the time, and used to send her 100R a month to lay out à discretion, and others from time to time combine with her. The best friend she has at present, is Mr Pusey who is here with his family for the benefit of his son's health. He is a Clergyman (brother of Dr Pusey) and tolerably rich, and very benevolent.

"Mary has very good health, and looks younger than she is, and is still pretty. She might have been advantageously married, but has never been disposed to change her estate, so that I suppose she will continue to form one of that half million of Englishwomen that there are more than men in the world. She is an excellent musician, but practises too little to be a brilliant performer and is nervous in company. This nervousness does not extend to the Church Services, which she performs admirably, and has been Organist here first at the Consular Chapel, and since Mr Lowe was turned out from there, at the Church at the Beco das Aranhas for 14 or 15 years."

Mary kept a diary from 1839 to 1843, recording her everyday pursuits. This diary is now in the Lambeth Archive and has been the subject of study by Cláudia Faria. She went to Newfoundland in 1859, spending more than a year with her brother Joe before he married. She visited Harriet in Natal in 1865/66, helping her through her sixth childbirth and organising the installation of better kitchen arrangements.

She was also an Associate of the Society of St Margaret, but after returning to England, lived at Clapham until her death in 1896, aged 73.

3 Anne (Kitty)   Born in Madeira 9 May 1824

"Kitty Anne is I think the <u>cleverest</u> of our daughters. Clever in conversation, clever in contriving, clever with her pen, clever with her needle. It is a mercy that she has so many resources as she is so constantly confined by ill health. With these, and with Arthur [her son] for a companion, she is never dull. I think her contentment under her many privations is one of her greatest merits. She is a pretty woman, but fat beyond all bounds. This is quite part of her complaint, and if ever her muscles and "solids" regain their tone, will no doubt subside in some measure, but both she and Bella are of the breed "unwieldy" which is a disadvantage through life, especially in old age. Anne's playing is almost as much admired as Fanny's – her finger is particularly spirited. How she happens to play at all, I can't think, debarred from touching the Piano (as at this time) for 1 or 2 years together as the case may be. She expects an addition to her family in November. If this event, thro' God's mercy, should not be again premature, we hope it may establish her health."

In an earlier letter, Elizabeth says of Anne "She is very useful to me as she entirely cultivates the garden in Town, which is an advantage for us all, and which I could not undertake to keep in order. And she has made herself a very good botanist, which one of every family ought to be, in a place so favourable for the cultivation of plants."

Anne's second child died soon after birth. She and her husband remained in Madeira after her parents left, taking their son Arthur to a school in England in 1865 and eventually establishing themselves in Middlesex. Anne died there in 1895, aged 70.

4 Fanny   Born in Kent 21 August 1826

At the age of 19 Fanny went to live with her maternal uncle, John Dickinson and his wife Ann. Originally the plan was for her to stay a year, but in fact she lived with them at Abbot's Hill, Hertfordshire or their London home, until her marriage, with only short holidays in Madeira. She was a faithful correspondent with her parents and siblings and also a conscientious keeper of family records.

"Fanny you <u>do</u> know tolerably, but it is not easy, without constant intercourse and observation, to realize the excellence of her different qualities. Temper – conduct – nous – industry – patience – cheerfulness. The rock she has split upon has been taking too little thought for herself. If, like Bella, she had laid down, and maintained a rule for such bodily indulgence as her physical temperament required, she might have preserved up to this time, the fine constitution which she had as a young girl. But though healthy, she was not tough, and has exerted herself in a manner disproportionate to the tenderness and delicacy of her frame. Fanny's playing is, as you are aware, as near perfection as is necessary in this imperfect world."

Her cousin, Jack Evans, lost his wife after

childbirth, leaving him with five small children. Fanny and Jack were married 18 months later in July 1859 and she became a much-loved step-mother. She had never been strong and was the first (and youngest) of the 11 children to die, aged 64, in 1890. Her oldest stepson was Sir Arthur Evans who excavated Knossos in Crete.

5 Harriet   Born in Kent 9 February 1828.

Harriet was often in charge of the education of her younger siblings, though she, like her sisters, had received her own education from her mother and visiting tutors. At the age of 26 in 1854, she married John Lake Crompton, an English clergyman who had come to Madeira for his health. She was the only one of the children to be married in Madeira, which necessitated a civil ceremony at the British Consulate, before the service in the English church, which was followed by a lavish reception. Three years later they settled in Pinetown in Natal.

"Harriet is different from the rest, though not inferior. Her principles are very high – rather of the severe kind, and her temper good, but she is less practical than her Sisters. Less handy, less attentive to the accessories of life. She is absent in mind, and indifferent to externals. You would say that she was the only one unsuited to a Settler's life, but this has not proved so. Her equable disposition carries her over difficulties which others might have combated, while her excellent understanding enables her to direct her attention to arts which do not come naturally, and, of course, to acquire them. She says she is an excellent cook, washer and ironer – professions as foreign to her nature as hunting truffles. Her philosophical disposition will save her from giving undue weight to those annoyances which of course always beset a Colonist's life, and she finds herself happy and contented amidst all its difficulties. She is, from nature, the best musician of the whole; consequently her performance is always charming to the lover of music but she has not a very brilliant finger. Her voice is extremely musical and her taste, perfect. She feels her author's meaning instinctively, so expresses it well. You may suppose how grateful and thankful I am to dear Aunt Grover for bestowing a beautiful new Piano upon her. It was really a <u>sin</u> for her to be without an Instrument, and I could not help feeling very angry with John for allowing her to be so, while he was spending his hundreds upon tracts of land. He is extremely fond of her, and entirely appreciates her music, but there is nothing graceful or engaging in his disposition and he would never think that a gratification to his wife could be a duty."

She was responsible for introducing many plants from Madeira, which are favourites in Natal gardens today. She was one of the pioneers of the Women's Movement in South Africa being the first president of the Pinetown Suffrage Society. She bore ten children, two of whom died in childhood, and after the death of her husband in 1889 she was able to make many voyages to England, sometimes visiting Madeira on the way. She died in Pinetown in 1925, aged 97.

6 Joseph Francis (Joe) born in Madeira 26 May 1829

The family hoped that Joe, the eldest son, would follow his father into the wine trade after completing his schooling with his uncle, Dr A. B. Evans. He did not show any inclination or aptitude for trade, however, and went to study theology at St Augustine's College, Canterbury. He went to Newfoundland (where there was a settlement of Portuguese speakers), was ordained there and served in the cathedral at St John's, the mission at Portugal Cove, as vice-principal of the theological college there and as headmaster of the Church of England School.

A letter in December 1853 says: "We have such charming letters from Joe, who doesn't mind the severity of his climate, though the lather freezes to his face as he shaves, and the water to his teeth as he brushes them. He is charmed because he is improving the Music at the Cathedral, in conjunction with his friend William having introduced "Helmore"[37] in the daily services in which there was formerly <u>no</u> music, (the Sunday services are not altered at present) and has got 12 volunteer boys to practise."

In September 1862 he married Fanny, daughter of Sir Bryan Robinson, a politician and judge in Newfoundland. They had nine children, two of whom died young. Their eldest son, Francis (Frank), became Bishop of Grahamstown and later Archbishop of Cape Town. In 1884 Joe and family moved to England, Joe taking up various clerical appointments to make ends meet, and eventually retired to Iffley, Oxford, where he died in 1922, aged 93.

7 Clara born in Madeira 19 February 1831.

Clara suffered from back trouble which was eventually cured by treatment in England. She spent a number of years living with her Phelps aunts and uncles in London, but it was at home in Madeira that she met John Oakley who had come to tutor the children of a local English family. Although they formed an attachment, he was not in a position to marry so they had a very long engagement. Clara's musical accomplishments were singing (coached by a visiting German professor) and playing the machete, a stringed instrument native to Madeira.

"Clara is clever and practical in an eminent degree. She has enough to do, having taken up Bella's part in the bordados, and having her own affairs also upon her mind. Her "young man" is an excellent young man – profoundly impressed with the awful responsibilities of his sacred calling. They keep up a frequent correspondence, but I do not see any prospect at present of a union. They have no intention of waiting till they are <u>rich</u> to be married, but they <u>must</u> have bread and cheese. Oakley Senior would probably double any little dowry that your Papa could bestow on Clara. She has a beginning in dear Aunt Page's library, which she has given her, and which has been sold for £120. The Papa has also given her 10 pipes of Wine."

She and John Oakley were eventually able to

marry in January 1860. He rose through the church hierarchy to become Dean of Carlisle and later Dean of Manchester. They had seven children and Clara died in England in 1897, aged 66.

8 Charles (Charlie)   born in Madeira 20 February 1833.

Charlie seems to have suffered quite severe hearing loss as a young man. He attended school in England and then worked for a time in the family business in Madeira. With the decline of the wine trade after the vines became diseased, there did not seem to be a future for him there so he was sent to Australia with a labourer from Madeira, where family friends had promised to help him get started. He took some wine to sell to provide capital and did purchase land and plant vines but these did not do well and he eventually became almost destitute and worked as a labourer on a sheep farm. He returned to England in 1862 and joined his uncles in their business in Rood Lane, London. In 1869 he married Sarah Agnes Neale who bore him a daughter, but Sarah died in 1876. He married Katherine Wilkinson in 1877. In old age he suffered from senile dementia and was cared for by a couple in Withernsea, Yorkshire where he died in 1908, aged 75.

9 William (Willie)   born in Madeira 23 January 1836

Willie attended Dr Evans's school in Market Bosworth but poor health interrupted this. He suffered from tuberculosis as a child causing an abscess on his leg which would flare up from time to time all his life. He returned home to Madeira and various tutors were found for him, but he was never able to make much progress and also had poor eyesight.

A letter of 1853 says: "Willy is out shooting all day. He sometimes brings home a Quail, sometimes a rabbit, and oftener 2 or 3 blackbirds. He is pretty well, now that he amuses himself all day."

He became engaged to a lady in Madeira who died before they were married, after which he was sent to join his brother Charlie in Australia. He ran into debt and generally behaved rather irresponsibly and returned to England with Charlie in 1862, where his parents hoped he would be accepted for a military career, the one occupation he wished for.

Quote from *Victorian Hangover* (by Frances Roper, born Hubbard): "At that time the sight test consisted merely of describing the view from the window of the examiner's room. Willie knew that this test would be far beyond his capacity and that he would certainly be rejected on that score. He therefore arranged with a friend entering at the same time, that the friend should go to the examiner ahead of him, and retail to him the necessary features of the view. When Willie's turn came he described the view, which to him was no more than a blur, with quite remarkable accuracy, and passed triumphantly into the Army."

Willie was eventually gazetted to the 2nd West India Regiment but later sold out. He married Catherine Glasse in 1870 and they had one stillborn daughter. For some time he and his wife cared for the children of his brother Arthur, while Arthur and his wife were in India. Letters written by his sister, Jane, in the 1890s suggest he was a neglectful husband, lavishing his time and money on the daughters of his brother Joe. He died at Droxford, Hants in 1911, aged 75.

10 Arthur   born in Madeira 24 October 1837

Arthur attended Dr Evans's school in Market Bosworth for almost six years, starting at the age of 9 and seeing his parents and siblings only when they visited England. Aged 15, he spent a year at Dr Bridgman's Academy, Woolwich, preparing for a career in the British East India Company's army. He went straight from there, in December 1853, to Bombay. He passed further examinations in Indian languages, surveying and civil engineering, serving in the Public Works department and the Commissariat, among various other appointments. During a period of leave in 1866, he paid a visit to his sister, Harriet in Natal. He married his second cousin, Caroline Peyton, in Bombay in 1868 and soon after was posted to Aden where their first two sons were born.

Carrie later bore him a daughter and another son, all the children spending much of their childhood with grandparents or uncles in England. He rose to be a General, retiring (with the rank of Lieutenant General) to Birmingham in the 1890s. He took up a number of interests, principally the anti-vaccination movement and was also a vegetarian. He died in Birmingham in 1920, aged

82 and his body was cremated, a procedure for which he was an early advocate.

11 Jane (Janey) born in Madeira 19 August 1842

Born five years after a string of three brothers, Janey was quite a tomboy and even when 15 was still climbing the mulberry tree. She had a donkey which she rode and also tried to teach to perform tricks. She was the only daughter to be sent to a formal school, Crieff College in Scotland, after which she spent some years in England, staying with her grandmother and aunt at Bramblebury. Like her sister Clara, she was sent to Mr Jago when she developed a weakness in her back, which was successfully treated.

"Janey is just what you remember her. Not in the least altered in countenance, only in stature. She is pretty, but has no pretensions to be called a beauty. The characteristic of her face is rather sweetness than beauty. She has her fair complexion and her beautiful hair, and a delicacy and refinement in the cast and expression of her features which is engaging. It is well she has, to counteract the effect of her "Tom-boy" propensities, which are as unchanged as the rest of her disposition. This is the Mulberry Season – and of all the frequenters of the tree, the most elevated among the branches, is always Janey. She is remarkably childish for her age (16 next week) and finds her amusements in playing with the kitten and moulding likenesses, but she is diligent and regular in the Schoolroom and indeed, docile in all respects.

"She does not however devour books in the manner that the rest of you do, and it is quite a refreshment to have a Miss Phelps who is not <u>over</u> literary. Another plaything with which she is much occupied now is the "Bandoline" or Portuguese Guitarre, strung with Wire. We have several of these old instruments in the house, so, out of sheer economy, I brought them to light, and found out an old Sergeant who knew how to play, and engaged him to teach her, and she takes her lessons under a Chestnut Tree and we are all charmed with the effect. It is not so good an instrument as the Machete, but makes a variety and is easier. Janey practises with diligence at the Piano, and I am thankful to say there is no longer any occasion to restrict her as to sitting up, as, from the closest observation we can give, we are satisfied that there is no weakness in her back. She is of a slenderer type than the rest, and perhaps more delicate in constitution, (though with invariably good health), as her appetite is smaller." Moving to England with her parents in 1861, she became aware that no provision was made by local authorities for children who had one parent living, or who simply were in bad homes. In her early twenties, she founded an Orphanage with her own money. From small beginnings the Orphanage grew rapidly, till for many years she had over a hundred children, and a big establishment in Kilburn. Later when public responsibility began to awaken, the numbers gradually diminished and she moved to a large house near Peckham Rye, housing about forty children.

Janey maintained a regular correspondence with her sister Harriet in Natal, and from these letters we see that she managed to lead quite a busy social life and kept contact with numerous members of the extended family, many of whom were drawn in to help with the orphanage and much-needed fund-raising events. Janey died at the orphanage in 1926, aged 84, leaving her estate to Ermenild Neale, Mother Superior of the Society of Saint Margaret, East Grinstead.

Joseph Phelps and his youngest daughter Janey.

[1] Madeira: the Island Vineyard by Noel Cossart. Christie's Wine Publications.
[2] maize meal
[3] James Sheffield worked for Joseph Phelps for many

years and attended to business while he was away.

[4] embroidery

[5] The girls' school which Elizabeth Phelps founded in Madeira was based on the "Lancaster System", whereby older pupils taught the younger ones.

[6] This would have been the 3rd Earl Nelson, a great nephew of the hero of Trafalgar.

[7] Lowe finally resigned in 1852, though he paid many more visits to Madeira to collect natural history samples.

[8] The Carmo Church was right opposite the house.

[9] barriga = belly

[10] Joseph's cousin, Abel Peyton, son of his mother's brother, was a manufacturing chemist in Birmingham.

[11] Lockjaw was a name commonly used for tetanus until at least the middle of the twentieth century.

[12] hut

[13] shepherds

[14] rested

[15] heather

[16] courage or resolution

[17] girls

[18] master

[19] Queen

[20] It will all be sorted out eventually. Silvestre Ribeiro (civil governor) supposed it was the Camara (City Hall) who had to deal with the consequences of the fire.

[21] sweets

[22] peasants

[23] Queen Adelaide, widow of King William IV.

[24] The title 'King of Holland' had been bestowed by Napoleon Bonaparte on his brother Louis who died in 1846. The man referred to here must be his son, who later became Napoleon III.

[25] Countess Julie von Egloffstein (1792 to 1869) a gifted amateur painter at the court.

[26] Thomas Heaphy, 1775 to 1835

[27] William Fishburn Donkin, professor of Astronomy

[28] Thomas Goodban, born at Canterbury about 1780 was author of some instruction books for the violin and pianoforte, and of 'The Rudiments of Music,' published about 1825. He was also the inventor of a 'Musical Game' for imparting elementary instruction, and of 'Musical Cards' for teaching the theory of music. He died in 1863.

[29] Cāndido de Vasconcelos published a collection of pieces for the machete in 1846.

[30] desfeita = slight

[31] farm

[32] The girls' school which Elizabeth Phelps founded in Funchal was based on the "Lancaster System", whereby older pupils taught the younger ones.

[33] Overseer

[34] About 5 miles (8 Km) from Funchal

[35] This appears to be a card game for three to five players.

[36] east wind

[37] Thomas Helmore was responsible for the revival of Gregorian chants in the Church of England.

||||| |||| ||| |||| || ||||| |||||||| ||| |||||||| ||| |||
80795755R00050

Made in the USA
Columbia, SC
22 November 2017